# H⊕PE
# IN THE END

## A 31-DAY JOURNEY THROUGH THE END-TIMES

## CYRIL OPOKU

*Hope in the End: A 31-Day Journey Through the End-Times*

Published by *Quest Publications (questpublications@outlook.com)*

Cover design & Interior layout by *Quest Publications*

ISBN: 978-1-988439-53-2
Printed in the United States of America

First Edition: June 2025

For more devotionals by BiblePlan™ Devotionals visit *TeenCompass Collective:* https://teencompasscollective.org

# Contents

## WEEK 4: Hope, Victory & the New Creation

# Author's Preface

When I first began studying the End-Times, I was overwhelmed. So many symbols, so much mystery, and countless opinions—some filled with fear, others with speculation. But as I spent time in Scripture, something shifted. I stopped trying to figure out every timeline and started focusing on the One who stands at the center of it all: Jesus Christ.

This devotional was born out of that journey. It's not a theological encyclopedia or a prediction of dates and events. It's an invitation. An invitation to draw closer to God, to wake up spiritually, and to live each day with a sense of urgency, hope, and obedience. The goal is not to become experts in prophecy but to become faithful disciples in practice.

Over these next 31 days, we'll walk through key passages that speak about the End-Times—from the warnings of Jesus, to the visions of Daniel, to the glory of Revelation. Each devotion is meant to be simple yet meaningful, grounded in Scripture, and focused on real-life application.

I pray that as you read, you'll not only gain understanding but experience transformation. That your heart will burn with love for Christ, your life will reflect His holiness, and your hope will be anchored in His return.

Because He is coming. And He calls us to be ready.

In Christ's service,
Cyril O.
*"Even so, come, Lord Jesus."* – Revelation 22:20

# Living in the Light of the End

W hat if you lived every day with the end in mind—not with fear, but with faith?

This 31-day devotional invites you to explore what Scripture says about the End-Times, not as a puzzle to decode, but as a promise to live by. Too often, discussions about the end of the world stir up anxiety or controversy. But for followers of Jesus, the end is not the end—it's the beginning of something far greater. Revelation, Daniel, Matthew, and other prophetic books weren't written to confuse us. They were given to prepare us, anchor our hope, and inspire holy living in a world that's rapidly shifting.

Each day, you'll walk through key passages that unveil God's ultimate plan, Christ's victorious return, and the call for believers to stay alert, faithful, and grounded in truth. Whether you're just curious about prophecy or longing for clarity in a chaotic world, this devotional will help you see Jesus more clearly—not only as Savior and Shepherd, but as soon-coming King and Judge.

You'll be encouraged to examine your heart, strengthen your faith, and look up—for your redemption draws near (Luke 21:28).

So take a deep breath, open your Bible, and lean in. These aren't just last days we're reading about—they're your days too. Let's live them well.

*"Blessed is the one who reads aloud the words of this prophecy, and blessed are those who hear, and who keep what is written in it, for the time is near."*— Revelation 1:3 (ESV)

*Day 1*

# Birth Pains and Bold Faith

**BiblePlan Reading:** Matthew 24:1–14

*"And this gospel of the kingdom will be preached in the whole world as a testimony to all nations, and then the end will come."*
— Matthew 24:14 (NIV)


Jesus' words in Matthew 24 are both sobering and hope-filled. As His disciples marveled at the grandeur of the temple, Jesus stunned them with a prophecy: *"Not one stone here will be left on another."* He then described signs of the end—the rise of false messiahs, wars and rumors of wars, natural disasters, persecution, betrayal, and increasing wickedness. These are not just random tragedies; Jesus called them "birth pains," signaling that something greater is coming: the arrival of God's kingdom in fullness.

This passage reveals God's sovereign control over history. He is not caught off guard by the chaos of our world. Instead, He has a plan unfolding—one that includes warning signs not to instill fear, but to prepare and awaken us. Amid global unrest and spiritual deception, one truth remains firm: the gospel will be preached to all nations.

No force of darkness, persecution, or indifference will stop God's plan of salvation from reaching the ends of the earth.

For believers, these verses are both a wake-up call and a word of comfort. While the world grows darker, we are called to remain steadfast in our love, anchored in truth, and actively sharing the good news. We must not be alarmed or distracted, but alert and faithful. Endurance is not passive survival—it is active trust and obedience, even when the cost is high.

You might feel overwhelmed by the instability around you, but Jesus reminds us: stay the course. Cling to Him. Proclaim hope. The gospel mission isn't finished yet—and you are part of it.

**Prayer:**

*Lord, help me not to be shaken by the chaos in the world. Teach me to endure, to love boldly, and to share Your gospel with courage and compassion. Strengthen my heart to stay faithful until the end. Amen.*

# Endurance in the Midst of Chaos

**BiblePlan Reading** – Matthew 24:15–35

*"Heaven and earth will pass away,*
*but my words will never pass away."*
—Matthew 24:35 (NIV)

When Jesus spoke about the "abomination of desolation" and the great tribulation to come, He wasn't just giving His disciples a prophetic timeline—He was preparing their hearts. This portion of Matthew 24 is both sobering and hope-filled. It reveals a future marked by deception, persecution, cosmic upheaval, and the ultimate return of the Son of Man. For many, these verses stir fear or confusion. But at the heart of Jesus' words is a clear call: remain alert, grounded, and faithful.

Jesus warned of false messiahs and counterfeit signs designed to lead people astray, even the elect. He urged His followers not to be deceived, not to panic, and not to chase after rumors. Why? Because when He returns, it will be unmistakable—like lightning that lights up the entire sky. The imagery is powerful and reminds us that God is not a God of confusion or secrecy. His plans are precise, sovereign, and sure.

God's character shines through this prophetic passage: He is just, merciful, and unshakably faithful. Despite the terrifying events described, we find great comfort in Jesus' promise that His words will never pass away. In a world that constantly shifts and crumbles, His truth stands forever. That means His promises of redemption, judgment, and final victory are not only certain—they are coming.

So how should we live today in light of tomorrow? We watch, we wait, and we walk in obedience. End-times prophecy isn't meant to make us paranoid, but prepared. It's a reminder that our hope isn't in this world, but in the One who is returning to make all things new.

## Prayer:

*Lord, in a world full of noise, chaos, and deception, help me to stay anchored in Your truth. Teach me to discern wisely, to live faithfully, and to long for Your return with hope—not fear. May Your Word be the foundation I build my life on, now and forever. Amen.*

# Stay Ready, Stay Awake

**BiblePlan Reading:** Matthew 24:36–51

*"Therefore you also must be ready, for the Son of Man is coming at an hour you do not expect."*
—Matthew 24:44 (ESV)

No one knows the day or hour when Jesus will return—only the Father. That's the sobering truth Jesus shares in this passage. Not the angels, not even the Son Himself while on earth—only God the Father holds that timing. Jesus paints a vivid picture of what life will be like before His return: normal, routine, and unassuming, just like the days of Noah. People will be eating, drinking, marrying—caught up in everyday life—when suddenly, judgment will come.

This isn't meant to scare us but to wake us up. The call to "stay awake" and "be ready" isn't about guessing dates or predicting signs; it's about living faithfully in every moment. Jesus goes on to describe two types of servants: the faithful one who stays ready and obedient while the master is away, and the careless one who acts as if the master's delay means he won't return anytime soon.

This reveals something crucial about God's heart. He is patient, giving us time to live wisely and draw near to Him. But He's also just—His promises, including judgment and reward, will come to pass. God's delays are not denials; they are grace-filled opportunities for repentance and preparation.

In a world where distractions are constant, Jesus invites us to focus on what truly matters: faithfulness. Whether we're washing dishes, leading a meeting, doing homework, or scrolling through our phones, we're called to live with the expectation that He could return at any moment. That's not a burden—it's a blessing. It means our choices matter, our obedience matters, and every moment is a chance to serve the King who will come again.

## Prayer:

*Lord, help me stay awake to what matters. Teach me to live each day with faithfulness, not fear. I want to be found ready, trusting You, and walking in obedience when You return. Keep my heart aligned with Your will and my eyes fixed on eternity. Amen.*

*Day 4*

# Hope Beyond the Clouds

**BiblePlan Reading:** 1 Thessalonians 4:13–18

*"For the Lord himself will come down from heaven, with a loud command, with the voice of the archangel and with the trumpet call of God, and the dead in Christ will rise first."*
—1 Thessalonians 4:16 (NIV)

In this passage, Paul reveals key truths about the return of Christ and the hope it brings believers. First, the Lord's return will be visible and unmistakable—He will come down from heaven with a loud command and trumpet call, not quietly or secretly. This shows God's power and authority over all creation.

Second, the "dead in Christ" will rise first. This means that believers who have died will be resurrected bodily, showing that salvation includes the whole person—body and soul. It highlights God's power over death and His promise of eternal life.

Third, those still alive will join with the resurrected believers "in the clouds" to meet the Lord together. This event is known as the

Rapture, where Christ gathers His Church to be with Him forever. It's a moment of hope and reunion for all believers.

Theologically, this passage teaches that death is not the end for Christians. God has a plan to restore and glorify His people fully. The return of Christ is both a promise and a motivation for believers to live holy, hopeful lives, eagerly anticipating that day.

## Prayer:

*Father, thank You for the hope of Jesus' return. Help me to live with confidence and joy, trusting in Your promise of eternal life. Amen.*

*Day 5*

# Watch and Be Ready

**BiblePlan Reading:** 1 Thessalonians 5:1–11

*"But you, brothers and sisters, are not in darkness so that this day*
*should surprise you like a thief. You are all children of the light and*
*children of the day. We do not belong to the night or to the darkness.*
*So then, let us not be like others, who are asleep,*
*but let us be awake and sober."*
—1 Thessalonians 5:4–6 (NIV)

P aul's words to the Thessalonian believers remind us about the certainty and unexpected nature of "The Day of the Lord," the time when Jesus will return to judge and redeem. Though no one knows the exact hour, God calls His people to live alert and prepared lives. The imagery of a thief coming in the night emphasizes how sudden and surprising this day will be for those who are unready. But Paul contrasts that with the believer's identity: as children of light, we are not meant to live in spiritual darkness or sleepiness.

This passage reveals God's loving desire for us to be awake, aware, and faithful until Christ returns. He doesn't want us caught off guard or overwhelmed by fear, but instead to live in hope and confidence, clothed in faith and love, and protected by the hope of salvation. It is a reminder that God's plan includes both judgment and salvation, and that living in light means reflecting His holiness and readiness.

For you, this means cultivating a daily posture of spiritual alertness. Are you living distracted or asleep to God's voice? Are you investing in faith, hope, and love in your everyday life? Preparing for the Lord's return is not just about waiting—it's about living intentionally in obedience and joy, knowing that God is sovereign and His promises are true. You can face the future without fear because you belong to the day, not the night.

## Prayer:

*Lord, help me to stay awake and sober in my faith. Guard my heart against complacency and fear. Fill me with Your hope and love as I wait for Your return. Strengthen me to live each day in readiness, shining Your light to the world. In Jesus' name, Amen.*

*Day 6*

# The Rise of the Man of Lawlessness

**BiblePlan Reading:** 2 Thessalonians 2:1–12

*"Don't let anyone deceive you in any way, for that day will not come until the rebellion occurs and the man of lawlessness is revealed, the man doomed to destruction."*
—2 Thessalonians 2:3 (NIV)

Paul's letter to the Thessalonians addresses a critical concern about the timing of the Lord's return. In this passage, he warns that before Christ's second coming, a powerful figure called "the man of lawlessness" will appear—a person who opposes God, sets himself up as divine, and deceives many. This figure symbolizes ultimate rebellion against God, characterized by lawlessness, false miracles, and lies. The passage reveals that God is sovereign, even over this time of deception and chaos. Though evil will rise, God's plan remains intact: the man of lawlessness will be exposed and judged in God's perfect timing.

This passage reminds us that spiritual deception is real and can be powerful. However, God has not left us helpless. He gives believers discernment through His Spirit and His Word to stand firm in the truth. The "man of lawlessness" serves as a signpost that the day of Christ's return is near, urging us to remain watchful and faithful.

For you today, this means living with spiritual alertness and confidence in God's ultimate victory. Don't be swayed by lies or fear the chaos around you. Instead, anchor yourself in Christ's truth, grow in obedience, and share the hope of His coming with others. This passage calls you to prepare your heart, guard your faith, and live ready for the Lord's return—knowing that God's justice and righteousness will prevail.

## Prayer:

*Lord, help me to stand firm in Your truth when the world around me grows confusing and deceptive. Strengthen my faith and guard my heart from lies, that I may live with hope and readiness for Your return. Amen.*

# The Coming New Day

**BiblePlan Reading:** 2 Peter 3:1–13

*"But in keeping with his promise we are looking forward to a new heaven and a new earth, where righteousness dwells."*

—2 Peter 3:13

The apostle Peter writes this letter to remind believers of the certainty and significance of "The Day of the Lord," a future time when God will bring final judgment and renew all things. Some scoffed at the promise of Christ's return, thinking everything would remain unchanged. But Peter urges us to remember that God's timing is perfect—what seems like delay is actually His patience, giving more people a chance to repent and be saved.

This passage reveals God's justice and mercy working hand in hand. He will not tolerate sin forever, but He also desires no one to perish. The earth as we know it will pass away, replaced by a glorious new creation where righteousness dwells. This new heaven and new earth is the ultimate hope for believers—a world free from pain, evil, and death.

For us today, this means we live with a purposeful anticipation. We do not live carelessly or in fear but with faithfulness and holiness, knowing that God is preparing a perfect future for those who love Him. We should be a people who encourage one another with this hope and who live as citizens of God's coming kingdom, reflecting His character here and now.

## Prayer:

*Father, thank You for Your patience and Your promise of renewal. Help me to live each day with hope and holiness, trusting in Your perfect timing and preparing my heart for the new creation You have prepared. Keep me faithful until that glorious day. In Jesus' name, Amen.*

*Day 8*

# The Glory of the Risen Christ

**BiblePlan Reading:** Revelation 1

*"When I saw him, I fell at his feet as though dead. But he laid his right hand on me, saying, 'Fear not, I am the first and the last, and the living one. I died, and behold I am alive forevermore, and I have the keys of Death and Hades.'"*
—Revelation 1:17–18 (ESV)

John's vision in Revelation 1 is breathtaking. The same Jesus who once walked the dusty roads of Galilee now stands in unapproachable glory — eyes blazing like fire, voice thundering like rushing waters, face shining like the sun. This is not the meek Lamb headed to the cross, but the victorious Son of Man, reigning in divine authority and splendor.

Jesus reveals Himself as the Alpha and Omega, the beginning and the end. He holds the keys of death and Hades — authority over life, judgment, and eternity itself. To a church facing persecution, this revelation was not meant to frighten, but to comfort and embolden. John, overwhelmed by the sight, falls down in awe. Yet Jesus reaches out, lays His hand on him, and says, "Fear not." What grace, that such power and majesty is also tender and near.

This picture of Christ prepares us for the end-times not just by informing us, but by transforming us. We are reminded that Jesus is not just part of our story — He is the center of it. In a world that feels unstable and uncertain, Revelation 1 anchors us in the unshakable truth of Christ's eternal reign. He is alive forevermore. He is in control. He is with His church.

Are you living today with a clear vision of who Jesus truly is? In the rush of life and the chaos of culture, don't reduce Him to a figure of the past or a distant Savior. He is the risen King — glorious, powerful, and worthy of your complete trust and obedience.

## Prayer:

Jesus, open my eyes to see You as You truly are — radiant in glory, reigning in power, and full of mercy. Help me live each day in awe of Your majesty and in surrender to Your will. You are alive forevermore — and I trust in You. Amen.

*Day 9*

# The Rider on the White Horse

**BiblePlan Reading:** Revelation 19:11–21

*"Then I saw heaven opened, and behold, a white horse! The one sitting on it is called Faithful and True, and in righteousness he judges and makes war."*
—Revelation 19:11 (ESV)

The vision in Revelation 19 is stunning and sobering. Heaven opens—and instead of peace or stillness, a mighty warrior appears. Jesus Christ, no longer the humble servant riding into Jerusalem on a donkey, now rides a white horse in royal and righteous victory. He comes not to suffer, but to rule. His name is "Faithful and True," and He judges with justice. His eyes blaze like fire, His robe is dipped in blood, and His name is "The Word of God."

This scene isn't symbolic poetry—it's prophecy. Jesus is returning, not just to reign but to conquer all evil, once and for all. The armies of heaven follow Him, but He alone carries the sword of judgment.

17

The beast, false prophet, and kings of the earth are no match for Him. The battle is swift. The outcome certain. Evil loses. Christ wins.

This vision of Christ reveals a vital part of God's character often overlooked: His justice. While God's love, mercy, and patience are real, so is His holiness. He doesn't wink at sin forever. He will bring final justice. For believers, this isn't a threat—it's a promise. Christ's return means evil won't have the last word. Every injustice, lie, and rebellion will be dealt with. He will reign in truth.

But it also challenges us. Are we living like He's coming soon? Are we standing with Christ now—before the battle begins? The time for choosing sides is now, not later. He comes for a pure Bride, a faithful people, a ready army. Our call is to live in obedience, to hope in His return, and to boldly stand on His side—even when the world mocks.

## Prayer:

*Lord Jesus, You are Faithful and True. Thank You that You are coming again to conquer evil and reign forever. Help me live each day in hopeful obedience, standing firmly on Your side. Make me ready for Your return. Amen.*

# Reigning with Christ

**BiblePlan Reading:** Revelation 20:1–6

*"Blessed and holy is the one who shares in the first resurrection! Over such the second death has no power, but they will be priests of God and of Christ, and they will reign with him for a thousand years."*
—Revelation 20:6 (ESV)

For many, Revelation 20 can feel mysterious—dragons, chains, thrones, and a thousand-year reign. But beneath the symbolism is a profound truth: God has a final, victorious plan, and His people are included in it.

In this passage, we see Satan bound for a thousand years while Christ reigns. This period, often called the *millennium*, highlights the triumph of Jesus and the vindication of His saints. Those who were faithful—especially those martyred for refusing to worship the beast—are raised to life and given the honor of reigning with Christ. This is called the "first resurrection." Over these, the "second death"—eternal separation from God—has no claim.

This shows us a stunning glimpse of God's justice and faithfulness. He doesn't forget those who suffer for His name. He doesn't overlook those who stand firm in a dark world. Instead, He honors them with roles of authority and intimacy in His kingdom. God is not only a Savior; He is a Rewarder.

In today's world, it's easy to be discouraged by evil, compromise, and spiritual apathy. But Revelation 20 reminds us: it's worth it to stay faithful. The trials of today are real, but so is the reign to come. If we belong to Christ—if we live with Him now—we will reign with Him then. That's not fantasy; it's our future.

So live with the end in mind. Don't fear what the world may take from you. Instead, prepare your heart, pursue holiness, and encourage others to endure. We're not just waiting—we're training to reign.

## Prayer:

*Lord Jesus, thank You for the promise of reigning with You. Strengthen my heart to remain faithful in a world full of compromise. Help me live today in light of Your coming kingdom. May my life bring You glory until the day I see You face to face. Amen.*

# The Final Verdict

**BiblePlan Reading:** Revelation 20:7–15

*"And if anyone's name was not found written in the book of life, he was thrown into the lake of fire."*
—Revelation 20:15 (ESV)

At the end of time, after Christ's millennial reign, Satan will be released for a final rebellion. It will end swiftly—fire from heaven will consume his forces, and the devil will be cast into the lake of fire, joining the beast and the false prophet. Then comes the great white throne judgment. Every person who has ever lived will stand before God. Books will be opened. Deeds will be reviewed. And one final book—the Book of Life—will determine each person's eternal destiny.

This is one of the most sobering passages in Scripture. It speaks of ultimate justice—perfect, holy, and irreversible. God is not only merciful and loving; He is also righteous and just. He doesn't overlook sin, but deals with it fully. For those who rejected Him, there is eternal separation. For those whose names are written in the Book of Life—those who have trusted Christ—there is eternal life.

This isn't meant to scare us into obedience but to awaken us to reality. The choices we make now have eternal consequences. God has patiently delayed judgment so more people have time to turn to Him (2 Peter 3:9). But a day is coming when delay will end. Today is the day of salvation.

As believers, this passage should stir urgency in our hearts—both to live holy lives and to share the gospel boldly. If we truly believe this final judgment is coming, how can we live casually or stay silent? Our hope is not in our good deeds but in Jesus, who took our judgment on Himself so our names could be written in His book.

## Prayer:

*Lord, awaken my heart to eternity. Help me live with urgency and hope, knowing that the final judgment is real. Thank You for the cross, where justice and mercy met. Keep me faithful, watchful, and bold to share the good news. In Jesus' name, amen.*

# King Above All Kings

**BiblePlan Reading:** *Daniel 7:9–14*

*"And to him was given dominion and glory and a kingdom, that all peoples, nations, and languages should serve him; his dominion is an everlasting dominion, which shall not pass away, and his kingdom one that shall not be destroyed."*
*— Daniel 7:14 (ESV)*

Daniel's vision in chapter 7 pulls back the curtain on heaven's throne room. The Ancient of Days—God the Father—is seated in blazing majesty, surrounded by fire and holiness, executing judgment with absolute authority. Thrones are set in place, not by human rulers, but by divine will. Then comes "one like a Son of Man," riding on the clouds, entering the presence of the Ancient of Days. This is no ordinary man—this is Jesus Christ, the Messiah, receiving from the Father eternal authority, glory, and a kingdom that will never be shaken or overthrown.

This powerful vision is not a myth or mystery—it's a prophetic declaration of Jesus' final victory. Long before Jesus walked the earth, Daniel saw the risen Christ, exalted in glory, ruling over every tribe, tongue, and nation. The "Son of Man" title Jesus often used to describe Himself was a direct reference to this prophecy, showing that He was the fulfillment of Daniel's vision.

For believers, this passage is a solid foundation of hope. While kingdoms rise and fall, and the world seems increasingly unstable, Jesus' dominion remains unshaken. The end-times aren't about chaos for God's people—they're about the unveiling of Christ's rightful rule. As His followers, we are not spectators—we are citizens of that everlasting kingdom, called to live with courage, faith, and holy expectation.

Are you ready for that kingdom? Are you living today in light of His coming reign? This vision challenges us to re-center our lives on the eternal King, not the temporary powers of this world. No matter what the headlines say, the throne in heaven is occupied—and Jesus will return to rule in righteousness.

## Prayer:

*Lord God, You are the Ancient of Days, and Jesus is the exalted Son of Man. Help me to live with holy confidence, trusting in Your eternal rule. Prepare my heart for Your coming kingdom, and make me faithful as I wait. In Jesus' name, Amen.*

# Shining Like the Stars Forever

**BiblePlan Reading:** *Daniel 12:1–13*

*"And those who are wise shall shine like the brightness of the sky above; and those who turn many to righteousness, like the stars forever and ever."*
—Daniel 12:3 (ESV)

In Daniel 12, we are taken to a moment of cosmic significance— the time of the end. This passage unveils a future marked by both great distress and great deliverance. It speaks of the resurrection of the dead: some to everlasting life, others to shame and everlasting contempt. For the faithful, it offers a breathtaking promise—those who lead others to righteousness will shine like the stars forever. It is one of the clearest Old Testament glimpses of resurrection and eternal reward.

This vision reminds us that God is not only the Sovereign Lord of history but also the God of final justice and eternal hope. He knows those who are His, and in the end, He will raise them up. Suffering, persecution, and even death are not the end of the story. God's plan includes a resurrection, a final reckoning, and a glorious reward for the wise and faithful.

Daniel is told to seal up the book—not because it's irrelevant, but because its full meaning would become clearer in the future. And although Daniel would not live to see these things come to pass, he is promised rest and resurrection at the appointed time.

For us today, Daniel's vision is both a warning and a comfort. We live in a world filled with uncertainty, conflict, and moral confusion. Yet God calls us to live wisely, to remain faithful, and to help others find the path of righteousness. Every small act of obedience, every word of truth spoken, every life pointed toward Christ—it matters. Eternally.

If you feel weary or unseen, remember: God keeps the faithful in His book of life. And one day, you will shine forever with Him.

**Prayer:**

*Lord God, help me to live wisely and faithfully in a world that often forgets You. Give me courage to lead others toward righteousness and strength to endure to the end. Thank You for the promise of resurrection and eternal life. Help me to keep my eyes on You and my heart fixed on Your Kingdom. Amen.*

*Day 14*

# Lifted Up, Coming Back

**BiblePlan Reading:** Acts 1:6–11

*"This same Jesus, who has been taken from you into heaven, will come back in the same way you have seen him go into heaven."*
—Acts 1:11b (NIV)

Jesus had finished His earthly ministry. He had died, risen, and spent forty days proving to His disciples that He was alive. Now, in this powerful scene in Acts 1, He ascends into heaven before their very eyes. But before going, He gives them a mission: *"You will be my witnesses..."* (v. 8). And just like that, He's gone—lifted up into the clouds. The disciples are left staring upward, perhaps stunned, until two angels appear with a message of incredible hope: *This same Jesus will come back.*

This moment is full of significance. First, it confirms Jesus' divine authority. He didn't just disappear—He ascended, glorified, lifted above the earth in power. It also signals the beginning of a new era: the age of the Church, powered by the Holy Spirit. But perhaps most compelling of all is the promise that He will return. Not "might." Not "possibly." He *will* come back.

That promise should anchor our lives today. In a world full of distraction, fear, and uncertainty, the return of Christ reminds us that history is going somewhere. God is not finished with this world, and He has not forgotten His people. Jesus is coming back—not as a humble servant, but as a reigning King. That reality should stir our hearts with both hope and urgency.

So how should we live in light of this? Like the disciples, we're called not to stand staring into the sky, but to live on mission—sharing the gospel, walking in obedience, and preparing our hearts. The return of Christ is not just a future event; it's a present motivation. We live *today* in light of *that day.*

## Prayer:

*Lord Jesus, thank You for the promise of Your return. Help me to live with hope, boldness, and purpose until You come again. Fill me with Your Spirit so I can be a faithful witness in this world. May my life reflect my longing for You. Amen.*

*Day 15*

# Always on Watch

**BiblePlan Reading:** Luke 12:35–48

*"You also must be ready, because the Son of Man will come at an hour when you do not expect him."*
—Luke 12:40 (NIV)

Jesus' words in Luke 12 are both urgent and tender. He paints the image of servants waiting for their master to return from a wedding banquet, dressed for action, lamps lit, alert and watchful. These aren't just poetic metaphors—they are calls to live ready. Ready for His return. Ready to serve. Ready to stay faithful even when no one else is watching.

The passage highlights two kinds of servants: those who stay faithful and prepared even in their master's absence—and those who become careless, thinking they've got time to waste. The first group is blessed when the master returns, so much so that the roles are reversed—the master himself serves them! But the second group is caught off guard and judged severely. Jesus isn't trying to scare us; He's calling us to live with purpose and urgency.

This shows us a glimpse of God's character: He is a just and merciful Master. He rewards faithfulness, even when it's quiet and unseen. But He also expects responsibility from those who know Him— *"From everyone who has been given much, much will be demanded"* (v. 48). Our knowledge of the truth makes us accountable to live it out.

In a world where distractions are constant and spiritual complacency is easy, Jesus' words shake us awake. He reminds us that our time is not endless and His return is certain. The exact moment? Unknown. But the command is clear: Be ready. This isn't about paranoia or fear. It's about faithful, hope-filled living. Are we walking in obedience today as if He could return tonight?

Maybe that means making things right with someone, breaking free from a sin you've let slide, or simply choosing to live each day with eternal perspective. If Jesus returned tomorrow, would He find you watching and ready—or spiritually asleep?

## Prayer:

*Lord Jesus, awaken my heart to the reality of Your return. Teach me to live with purpose, obedience, and joyful expectation. Help me to stay faithful in the small things, even when no one is watching. I want to be ready when You come. Amen.*

*Day 16*

# Stay Awake

**BiblePlan Reading:** Mark 13:1–37

*"Therefore stay awake—for you do not know when the master of the house will come, in the evening, or at midnight, or when the rooster crows, or in the morning."*
—Mark 13:35 (ESV)

Jesus' words in Mark 13 are sobering and urgent. As He leaves the temple for the last time, His disciples admire the magnificent buildings, but Jesus warns that not one stone will be left on another. This sparks a larger conversation about the signs of the end times—the coming tribulations, false messiahs, cosmic disturbances, and ultimately, the return of the Son of Man.

The heart of Jesus' message isn't to stir fear, but to awaken His followers to watchfulness. He doesn't give dates or timelines, because the focus isn't on prediction—it's on preparation. The warning is clear: don't be caught sleeping. Be alert. Be faithful. Live as if Christ could return at any moment—because He can.

This passage reveals God's mercy and justice. In His mercy, He warns us in advance. He wants none to perish, but all to be ready. In His justice, He assures us that evil will not last forever—judgment will come, and Christ will reign. We're not called to live in panic, but in hopeful vigilance. This isn't a doomsday message; it's a call to live with purpose.

For believers, this changes everything. We don't chase the temporary. We invest in what lasts—eternal things. We keep our hearts clean, our hands busy with good, and our eyes fixed on Jesus. Watching doesn't mean staring at the sky—it means walking in holiness, speaking the gospel boldly, and living like citizens of heaven.

So what does it mean for you, right now? It means staying spiritually awake: guard your heart, stay in the Word, don't get numb to sin, and live with joyful expectation. The Master's return isn't a threat—it's our blessed hope. Be ready.

**Prayer:**

*Lord, awaken my heart to Your truth. Keep me alert, faithful, and full of hope as I wait for Your return. Help me not to be distracted or discouraged, but to live every day with eyes fixed on You. Come quickly, Lord Jesus. Amen.*

*Day 17*

# Equipped for the End

**BiblePlan Reading** – 2 Timothy 3:1–17

*"All Scripture is breathed out by God and profitable for teaching, for reproof, for correction, and for training in righteousness, that the man of God may be complete, equipped for every good work."*
—2 Timothy 3:16–17 (ESV)

In his final letter to Timothy, the apostle Paul paints a sobering picture of the last days—"perilous times" filled with godlessness, deception, and spiritual compromise. The chapter reads like a mirror to our modern world: people will be lovers of self, arrogant, unholy, and hostile to truth. Yet, in the middle of this chaos, Paul doesn't tell Timothy to hide or panic—he tells him to stand firm and to *continue in what he has learned* (v. 14).

What is the anchor in such times? The Word of God. Paul makes it clear that Scripture isn't just a book of moral stories—it is *God-breathed*. It carries His authority, His wisdom, and His transforming power. It teaches us truth, confronts our wrong thinking, corrects our paths, and trains us to live like Christ. God's Word is His personal provision for His people to remain faithful when the world grows dark.

This passage reveals the foresight and faithfulness of God. He knew perilous times would come, and He didn't leave us vulnerable. He gave us His Word—not just to survive, but to thrive. His plan has always been to shape a people who are rooted in truth, strong in faith, and ready for every good work.

For those who love Jesus, this is a call to wake up, press in, and hold fast. In a world that is increasingly hostile to truth, Scripture isn't optional—it's essential. Now is the time to grow in it, live by it, and share it boldly. Perilous times aren't the end of hope—they are the proving ground for a faithful life.

## Prayer:

*Father, thank You for the gift of Your Word. In these confusing and dangerous times, help me to stand firm in truth, to live by Your wisdom, and to be ready for every good work You have prepared for me. Teach me, shape me, and use me to shine Your light in the darkness. In Jesus' name, amen.*

# Stay Standing in a Falling World

**BiblePlan Reading:** Jude 1:17–25

*"But you, beloved, building yourselves up in your most holy faith and praying in the Holy Spirit, keep yourselves in the love of God, waiting for the mercy of our Lord Jesus Christ that leads to eternal life."*
— Jude 1:20–21 (ESV)

In these last days, when truth is often twisted and love grows cold, Jude's words are a call to spiritual alertness and perseverance. He warns of scoffers—those who follow ungodly desires, create division, and live without the Spirit. But Jude doesn't leave believers helpless. Instead, he gives clear instructions: *build yourselves up in your most holy faith, pray in the Holy Spirit, keep yourselves in God's love,* and *wait for Jesus' mercy.*

This passage reminds us that the Christian life, especially in difficult times, requires intention. Our faith must be strengthened daily—through God's Word, through community, and through Spirit-led prayer. God has not abandoned us in the chaos; He empowers us to stand firm.

Jude also reveals the heart of God: a Father who keeps us from stumbling and will present us *blameless with great joy*. He is both able and willing to preserve us. His plan isn't for fear but for faithfulness. He doesn't just save us once—He sustains us to the end.

As we see spiritual compromise increasing around us, our job is not to hide in fear but to stay rooted in truth, active in mercy, and grounded in hope. We must contend not only for the faith but for the souls of others—showing compassion, even to those on the edge of destruction (v. 22–23).

So don't be discouraged by the darkness. Be equipped in the Spirit. Keep your eyes on Jesus, your heart anchored in love, and your life aligned with eternal truth.


## Prayer:

*Father, strengthen me to stand firm in these last days. Help me to grow in faith, walk in Your love, and be led by Your Spirit. Keep me from falling, and use me to reach others with Your mercy. In Jesus' name, amen.*

# Wake-Up Call

### BiblePlan Reading – Romans 13:11–14

*"And do this, understanding the present time: The hour has already come for you to wake up from your slumber, because our salvation is nearer now than when we first believed."*
—Romans 13:11 (NIV)

Time is ticking. Paul's message to the Romans is urgent—like an alarm sounding in the early hours. He's not just talking about physical sleep, but spiritual drowsiness. It's the kind of sluggishness that slowly creeps in when we get too comfortable with the world, too distracted by routine, or too numb to the reality that Christ is coming back. Paul's call is simple: *Wake up.* The night is almost over. The dawn of eternity is about to break.

In this passage, Paul reminds believers that Jesus' return is closer now than it's ever been. That's not meant to scare us—it's meant to stir us. God isn't distant or disengaged; He's actively drawing history to a close. He's already given us the light—Jesus Christ—and now

He calls us to live like people who belong to the day, not the darkness.

What does that look like? It means turning away from the things that numb our spirits—sinful habits, selfish desires, and meaningless distractions—and instead clothing ourselves with Christ. We don't just believe in Him; we live like Him. Every choice, every attitude, every action should reflect the hope we have and the holiness we're called to.

Paul's urgency is our invitation to live awake—to be alert, watchful, and intentional in how we live each day. Whether Jesus returns tomorrow or a thousand years from now, we're called to live like He's coming today. This isn't about fear—it's about focus. The time for half-hearted faith is over. The time to shine, to love, to stand firm, to walk in purity—that time is now.

## Prayer:

*Lord, open my eyes to the times I'm spiritually asleep. Help me throw off the distractions and sins that dull my heart. Teach me to live with urgency, purity, and purpose, clothed in Christ and filled with hope. Keep me awake and ready for Your return. In Jesus' name, Amen.*

*Day 20*

# Hold Fast or Fall Away

**BiblePlan Reading:** Hebrews 10:23–31

*"Let us hold unswervingly to the hope we profess, for he who promised is faithful."*
—Hebrews 10:23 (NIV)

We live in a world of shifting values and uncertain promises. But God's Word offers something radically different—an unchanging call to remain steadfast in faith. Hebrews 10:23–31 is both a source of deep encouragement and a sober warning. The encouragement? We have a faithful God who keeps every promise. The warning? If we willfully turn from Him after knowing the truth, the consequences are serious.

This passage calls believers to stand firm in their hope, not just in words, but in action. The author urges us to keep gathering, keep encouraging one another, and stay spiritually awake—especially as the Day of Christ's return draws nearer. The picture is of a community clinging tightly to their shared hope, not letting go despite growing pressure and persecution.

But the passage also turns sharply serious. Deliberate sin after receiving the knowledge of truth is described as trampling the Son of God and insulting the Spirit of grace. That's not just moral failure—it's betrayal. God is loving and faithful, yes, but He is also just and holy. He's not a passive bystander to rebellion; He is the righteous Judge who sees everything clearly.

This tension between mercy and justice points us to God's full character. He longs for us to walk closely with Him and never give up—but He also will not be mocked or ignored. In light of eternity, every decision we make matters. Our faith must not be casual, but committed.

If you've drifted, today is the day to come back. If you're weary, now is the time to strengthen your grip on hope. The One who promised is faithful. Will you be?

## Prayer:

*Faithful Father, thank You for Your unshakable promises and unmatched mercy. Help me to hold tightly to the hope I have in Christ, even when the world around me pulls in every direction. Keep me from growing cold or careless. I don't want to drift—I want to stand. Help me honor You with my life, with reverence and with joy, until the day You return. In Jesus' name, Amen.*

# Wake Up and Hold On

**BiblePlan Reading:** Revelation 3:1–13

*"Wake up! Strengthen what remains and is about to die, for I have found your deeds unfinished in the sight of my God."*
— Revelation 3:2 (NIV)

The letters to the churches in Sardis and Philadelphia could not be more different. Sardis had a reputation for being alive, but in reality, Jesus calls them dead. They looked the part but had no spiritual pulse. They were asleep—spiritually careless, slowly wasting away. Jesus warns them to wake up, repent, and return to Him while there's still time.

Philadelphia, however, is praised for their faithfulness. Though they had "little strength," they had not denied Jesus' name. Because of their perseverance, Jesus promises to keep them safe during the trial that will come upon the whole world. He assures them that their faithfulness will be rewarded with eternal security in God's presence.

These two letters together paint a vivid picture of what it means to live awake and ready. Sardis shows us that reputation means nothing if we aren't rooted in Christ. God sees through appearances. Philadelphia reminds us that endurance—even when we feel weak—matters deeply to God. He honors those who remain true, even when it's hard.

God's message is clear: He wants His people alert and faithful. The end times will test our hearts. We can't afford to drift spiritually or live off yesterday's passion. Whether we feel strong like warriors or weak like survivors, what matters is that we cling to Jesus, obey His Word, and watch for His return.

So ask yourself—are you awake or coasting through your faith? Are you holding fast, or barely holding on? Jesus offers strength to the weary and revival to the spiritually dry. But we must respond while there's still time.

## Prayer:

*Lord Jesus, open my eyes where I've grown sleepy in my faith. Revive what's fading, and help me to cling to You with endurance. Like the church in Philadelphia, may I remain faithful, even when I feel weak. Help me live ready, watching and obeying until the day You return. In Your name, Amen.*

*Day 22*

# When All Things Are Made New

**BiblePlan Reading:** Revelation 21:1–8

*"He will wipe away every tear from their eyes. There will be no more death or mourning or crying or pain, for the old order of things has passed away."*
—Revelation 21:4 (NIV)

The book of Revelation often feels overwhelming with its vivid images of judgment, beasts, and battles. But in chapter 21, the tone shifts dramatically. The storm has passed. Evil has been defeated. And now, the apostle John is shown a breathtaking vision of what comes next: a new heaven and a new earth, where God Himself will dwell with His people forever.

This isn't just a spiritual concept—it's a literal transformation of everything we know. The old, broken world, scarred by sin and suffering, will be completely remade. God doesn't just patch things up. He starts fresh. And in that new creation, there is no room for sorrow, pain, or death. All the grief we've carried will be wiped away—not just eased, but erased.

What does this reveal about God? He is not distant. He is not indifferent to our tears. Instead, He is the kind of God who kneels down to wipe them away. He is a restorer, a rebuilder, and a Father who longs to bring His children home.

But this promise is not automatic for everyone. Verses 7 and 8 remind us that only those who overcome—those who remain faithful to Christ—will inherit this hope. The new world is for the redeemed. For those who refuse God's grace, there is a sobering warning.

In a world full of chaos and uncertainty, this passage calls us to prepare—not with panic, but with purpose. How we live now matters. Our obedience, our endurance, and our relationship with Jesus today shape our future forever. Let this vision fill you with hope and move you to live like someone who's headed for the New Jerusalem.

**Prayer:**

*Father, thank You for the promise of a new heaven and a new earth. When the world feels heavy, remind me that this is not the end of the story. Help me to live with eternity in mind—to walk in obedience, cling to hope, and trust Your plan. Prepare my heart for that day when all things are made new. In Jesus' name, Amen.*

Day 23

# Glory You Can't Imagine

**BiblePlan Reading:** Revelation 21:9–27

*"The city does not need the sun or the moon to shine on it, for the glory of God gives it light, and the Lamb is its lamp."*
—Revelation 21:23 (NIV)

Heaven isn't just a concept or a dreamy hope—it's a promised reality more stunning than our minds can grasp. Revelation 21 gives us a glimpse of what's coming: the New Jerusalem, the eternal home of God's people. This isn't just the end of the story; it's the ultimate beginning. A radiant city filled with beauty, purity, and God's overwhelming presence.

John is taken by an angel to see the "Bride, the wife of the Lamb," which is the city itself—perfect, holy, descending from heaven. Its brilliance is like that of a precious jewel. There are twelve gates, twelve foundations, streets of gold so pure they're like glass. But what stands out isn't the gold or the gemstones—it's that there's no temple in this city. Why? Because *God* and *the Lamb* are its temple. And there's no need for the sun or moon, because *God's glory lights it up.*

This passage reveals the heart of God's plan: not just to save us from sin but to bring us home to live with Him, forever. It's a vision of intimate, unbroken fellowship with the Creator. No more barriers, no more darkness, no more sin. Just God's people, God's light, and God's glory.

So what does this mean for us today? It means we're not living for this world—we're living for *that* one. The things we chase—status, comfort, control—are shadows compared to the eternal reality waiting for us. If the New Jerusalem is our forever home, then obedience and faithfulness today are acts of preparation. Hope isn't a feeling—it's an anchor.

When you're tired of the darkness of this world, remember the city that needs no sun.

## Prayer:

*Lord, thank You for the promise of the New Jerusalem. When the world feels dark, remind me of the light that is coming—Your eternal glory. Help me live today in preparation for forever with You. Strengthen my hope, purify my heart, and guide my steps until I see You face to face. In Jesus' name, Amen.*

Day 24

# Come, Lord Jesus!

**BiblePlan Reading:** Revelation 22:1–21

*"He who testifies to these things says, 'Yes, I am coming soon.'*
*Amen. Come, Lord Jesus."*
—Revelation 22:20 (NIV)

The final chapter of the Bible is not just an ending—it's a promise. Revelation 22 paints a breathtaking picture of what's to come: the river of life flowing from the throne of God, the tree of life bearing fruit for healing, and the radiant presence of the Lamb lighting up the eternal city. Everything broken will be restored. Everything dark will be gone. And at the center of it all is Jesus, declaring, "I am coming soon."

These words are both a promise and a call. Jesus isn't just offering comfort; He's inviting us to live expectantly. This chapter is filled with urgency. Three times Jesus says, "I am coming soon," and each time, it's meant to stir something in us—hope, awe, and readiness.

We live in a world where "soon" often feels far away. Wars rage, injustice lingers, and sorrow touches every life. But Revelation 22 reminds us that history is moving somewhere. God is not slow in keeping His promise. He is preparing a place where His people will see His face, where there will be no more curse, and where He will reign forever.

This passage reveals God's deep desire to dwell with us, to wipe away every tear, and to bring full redemption. It also challenges us to be ready—faithful, watching, and awake. We don't know the exact time, but we do know the end of the story. And we can live today in light of that glorious tomorrow.

So how do we wait? Not passively, but actively. We hold on to His words. We walk in obedience. We invite others into this hope. And above all, we pray with longing, like John: *"Come, Lord Jesus."*

**Prayer:**

*Lord Jesus, thank You for the promise that You are coming soon. Help me to live with hope, to walk in Your ways, and to keep my eyes fixed on eternity. When the world feels dark, remind me of the light that's coming. Fill me with urgency, not fear. Make me ready. Come, Lord Jesus. Amen.*

*Day 25*

# When Everything Is Made New

**BiblePlan Reading:** Isaiah 65:17–25

*"See, I will create new heavens and a new earth. The former things will not be remembered, nor will they come to mind."*
—Isaiah 65:17 (NIV)

C an you imagine a world where sorrow is erased, death is distant, and peace reigns not just between people, but even among animals? That's the stunning picture God gives us through Isaiah—a future reality where all things are made new. Isaiah 65:17–25 is more than poetic hope; it's a divine promise. God is not only going to fix what is broken—He's going to recreate everything into something far better than we've ever known.

In this vision, God speaks of a time when His people will live in joy and safety. No more tragic deaths, no more fruitless labor, no more fear. Children will grow old, people will enjoy the work of their hands, and even the natural world will reflect God's peace. The lion will eat straw like an ox, and the serpent—once a symbol of evil—

will no longer be a threat. This is not just an ideal future; it's God's declared intention for His redeemed creation.

This passage reveals the depth of God's love and the scope of His redemptive plan. He is not content to patch up the old. He plans to replace it with something entirely new—a world unmarred by sin, pain, and death. This reflects His faithfulness and power to bring ultimate restoration.

For us today, this passage is both comfort and calling. It reminds us that no matter how broken the present world feels, something better is coming. We are not meant to place our hope in temporary things. Instead, we prepare our hearts for eternity. We obey, not out of fear, but because we belong to the One who is making all things new. In the face of anxiety, injustice, or loss, we hold on to this promise: the best is yet to come.

## Prayer:

*Lord, thank You for the promise of a new heaven and a new earth. When this world feels heavy, remind me of what You're preparing. Help me to live with eternal hope, walking in obedience and trust. Make my life a preview of Your coming peace. In Jesus' name, Amen.*

*Day 26*

# The Ache of Hope

**BiblePlan Reading:** Romans 8:18–25

*"I consider that our present sufferings are not worth comparing with the glory that will be revealed in us."*
—Romans 8:18 (NIV)

The Apostle Paul paints a powerful picture in this passage—one of waiting, groaning, and eager longing. All of creation, not just humanity, is described as yearning for redemption, like a woman in labor waiting for new life to break through the pain. The world is broken. We feel it every day—in sickness, disasters, injustice, grief, and weariness. But Paul reminds us that this ache isn't empty; it's pregnant with promise.

Creation groans because it remembers something better, and it knows something greater is coming. Paul urges us to hold onto that hope: the future glory that will be revealed in us when Jesus returns. This isn't just a band-aid for hard times. It's the backbone of Christian endurance. The pain we feel now, whether physical, emotional, or spiritual, is real—but it's not permanent.

This passage reveals the heart of God: He hasn't abandoned His creation. He has a plan to redeem it fully. God isn't just going to rescue our souls—He's going to restore everything: our bodies, the earth, and the harmony between all things. He's a God who finishes what He starts. And right now, we live in the "already, but not yet"— redeemed by Christ, but still waiting for the fullness of that redemption to arrive.

For believers, this waiting isn't passive. It's hopeful and purposeful. We don't hope like the world does, fingers crossed, uncertain. Our hope is rooted in the faithfulness of God. We groan, but we also lean forward. We hurt, but we also hold on. Especially in the context of the end times, when the world seems more chaotic than ever, this passage reminds us that our eyes must stay fixed on the horizon. Jesus is coming. Glory is coming. And it will be worth it.

## Prayer:

*Father, thank You that my suffering is not the end of the story. When the weight of this world feels too much, help me remember that You are making all things new. Fill me with patient hope and trust in Your timing. Keep my eyes on Jesus, and teach me to live today in light of forever. In His name I pray, Amen.*

*Day 27*

# Home Is Already Waiting

**BiblePlan Reading:** John 14:1–7

*"Let not your hearts be troubled. Believe in God; believe also in me. In my Father's house are many rooms. If it were not so, would I have told you that I go to prepare a place for you?"*
—John 14:1–2 (ESV)

The night before Jesus went to the cross, He spoke words of deep comfort to His disciples. Their world was about to be turned upside down, and Jesus knew it. He didn't give them a strategy or escape plan—He gave them a promise. He said, "I go to prepare a place for you."

This wasn't just about heaven in the distant future—it was about trust in the present. Jesus saw the fear in their hearts, and He sees ours too. In a world filled with chaos, confusion, and the constant unknown, He says, "Let not your hearts be troubled." Why? Because our future is not up in the air. It's already secured.

Jesus is not just building a place—we're not just getting a room with our name on it. He's preparing *home*. A place where sin, suffering, and death are no more. A place with Him. The greatest part of heaven isn't gold streets or eternal life—it's Jesus. And He makes that clear when He says, "I am the way, and the truth, and the life. No one comes to the Father except through me."

That means our hope isn't based on how well we perform, how much we understand, or how strong we feel. Our hope is anchored in the One who went ahead of us, died for us, rose again, and is coming back for us. For believers, the End Times aren't something to fear— they're something to prepare for with hope. Jesus isn't just coming back for the world—He's coming back for *you*.

So keep your eyes up. Your heart can be at peace, even when the world is not. Because Jesus has already taken care of the hardest part. Your forever home is real—and it's ready.

## Prayer:

*Jesus, thank You for preparing a place for me. When fear creeps in and the world feels uncertain, remind me that my hope is secure in You. Help me live each day with confidence, peace, and purpose, knowing that my true home is with You forever. In Your name, Amen.*

*Day 28*

# Death Is Not the End

**BiblePlan Reading:** 1 Corinthians 15:20–28

*"But Christ has indeed been raised from the dead, the firstfruits of those who have fallen asleep."*
—1 Corinthians 15:20 (NIV)

Jesus rising from the dead wasn't just a miracle—it was a promise. His resurrection was the *firstfruits*, the beginning of something greater still to come. In this passage, Paul paints a sweeping picture of God's plan from creation to the final victory: through Adam came death, but through Christ comes resurrection. And not just for Him—but for all who belong to Him.

This is more than theology—it's our ultimate hope. The enemy called death, which has haunted humanity since Eden, is already defeated. It may still touch our lives now, but its days are numbered. Jesus's resurrection was the start of a domino effect that will end with every enemy under His feet, including death itself. God's plan is total and unstoppable. Nothing will stand in the way of His kingdom being fully established—where there will be no more sorrow, no more graves, no more tears.

This passage also reveals God's incredible order. Christ rose first. Then, when He returns, those who belong to Him will rise. After that, He will hand everything over to the Father. This is not chaos; this is divine choreography. God is not guessing His way through history—He's leading it, step by step, toward total restoration.

So what does this mean for us today? It means we don't have to fear death. It means every moment of obedience, every step of faith, every tear shed in the fight against sin is worth it. The end of our story is not darkness—it's glory. In a world still broken by sin and pain, we live as people who know how the story ends: Christ wins. Death dies. And we live forever.

## Prayer:

*Risen Savior, thank You for defeating death and giving me hope that lasts forever. Help me to live with courage and confidence, knowing that the final victory is already Yours. When I face fear or grief, remind me of what's coming—Your kingdom, Your glory, and life without end. In Jesus' name, Amen.*

# Victory Beyond the Grave

**BiblePlan Reading:** 1 Corinthians 15:50–58

*"Listen, I tell you a mystery: We will not all sleep, but we will all be changed— in a flash, in the twinkling of an eye, at the last trumpet. For the trumpet will sound, the dead will be raised imperishable, and we will be changed."*

—1 Corinthians 15:51-52 (NIV)

P aul's words in this passage reveal one of the greatest mysteries and hopes of the Christian faith: the resurrection of the dead and the transformation of the living at Christ's return. Our natural bodies, subject to decay and death, cannot inherit the eternal kingdom. Instead, God promises a radical change—our mortal, perishable bodies will be replaced by immortal, imperishable ones. This mystery is not just a future hope but a guarantee anchored in the resurrection of Jesus Christ Himself.

Through this resurrection, God demonstrates His power over death and His unwavering commitment to redeem all who trust in Him. Death, the final enemy, will be destroyed forever, giving believers victory and freedom from fear. This truth is foundational to our faith and shapes how we live now. Knowing that our present struggles and even death itself will not have the last word gives us courage and perseverance.

In a world that often feels uncertain and overwhelming, this passage invites us to stand firm in our faith and continue doing God's work with confidence and joy. We live in the "already" of Christ's victory but also the "not yet" of full resurrection and restoration. This tension calls us to be spiritually alert, obedient, and hopeful, reminding us that our labor for the Lord is never in vain.

As you face your daily challenges, remember that your ultimate destiny is secure, and your present life is part of a bigger, victorious story. Let this hope shape your attitude, your actions, and your readiness to meet Christ whenever He returns.

## Prayer:

*Heavenly Father, thank You for the hope of resurrection and the promise of eternal life. When I face fear or weariness, remind me that death has been defeated and that You have prepared a glorious future for me. Help me to stand firm, work faithfully, and live boldly, trusting in Your victory. In Jesus' name, Amen.*

*Day 30*

# Citizens of a Greater Kingdom

**BiblePlan Reading:** Philippians 3:17–21

*"But our citizenship is in heaven. And we eagerly await a Savior from there, the Lord Jesus Christ."*
—Philippians 3:20 (NIV)

In his letter to the Philippians, Paul reminds believers of their true identity: they are not first and foremost citizens of Rome—or any earthly nation—but citizens of heaven. This truth was a bold declaration in a city like Philippi, where Roman citizenship was a prized status. Yet Paul directs the church to lift their eyes higher and remember their eternal allegiance.

Paul contrasts those who live as "enemies of the cross of Christ" with those who follow the example of Christ and His apostles. The former are focused on earthly things—comfort, indulgence, status—while the latter live with heaven in view. Paul's call is clear: imitate those who walk faithfully with Jesus, for they are the ones heading in the right direction.

This passage reveals God's plan to transform us, not merely in behavior but in being. As citizens of heaven, we await a Savior who will return—not as a suffering servant, but as a conquering King. Christ will transform our "lowly bodies" to be like His "glorious body." This shows us that God's plan isn't only to save our souls, but to redeem and glorify our whole selves in the resurrection.

In a world growing increasingly uncertain, this truth gives deep hope. When we feel out of place or discouraged by the moral decline around us, we must remember that we're not home yet. Our true homeland is not found in earthly nations, but in the kingdom of God. Living as citizens of heaven means aligning our values, choices, and hopes with eternity—not the temporary systems of this world.

So today, walk with eternity in view. Let the hope of Christ's return shape your obedience now. Prepare your heart, your character, and your witness—because heaven is not only your destination, it's your identity.

**Prayer:**

*Lord Jesus, thank You for making me a citizen of heaven. Help me to live with eternity in my heart and to follow Your example in everything I do. Let my life reflect the hope of Your return and the glory of the kingdom to come. Amen.*

*Day 31*

# Grace on the Horizon

**BiblePlan Reading:** Titus 2:11–14

*"For the grace of God has appeared that offers salvation to all people. It teaches us to say 'No' to ungodliness and worldly passions, and to live self-controlled, upright and godly lives in this present age, while we wait for the blessed hope—the appearing of the glory of our great God and Savior, Jesus Christ."*
—Titus 2:11–13 (NIV)

The grace of God isn't just a soft cushion for our mistakes—it's a powerful, transformative force that trains us how to live. In Titus 2, Paul reminds us that grace has appeared to offer salvation to all, but it doesn't stop at forgiveness. Grace becomes our teacher, shaping our lives today as we await the return of Jesus.

This passage draws a straight line from salvation to sanctification to expectation. First, God's grace saves us—freely, undeservedly, and fully. Then it teaches us to live differently—to say "no" to what drags us down and "yes" to what honors God. But perhaps most importantly, it gives us a reason to live with hope. We're not just surviving this world; we're waiting for the return of our Savior, who will come again in glory.

God's plan is both present and future. Right now, He's making us more like Jesus—training us in holiness and good works. But at the same time, He's preparing to return. That hope—His glorious appearing—shapes how we live today. Knowing He is coming again gives purpose to our obedience, strength to our struggles, and clarity to our waiting.

In a culture that's always rushing forward or falling apart, this passage calls us to live grounded in grace and anchored in hope. The world says "do what feels good now." God says, "Live today like I'm coming tomorrow."

## Prayer:

*Lord, thank You for Your saving grace and for the hope of Your return. Teach me to live with purpose, resisting what pulls me away from You and embracing the life You've called me to. Help me wait well—not passively, but actively—becoming more like Christ as I hope in Your promise. Amen.*

*Epilogue*

# Until He Comes

We've reached the end of this 31-day journey—but in many ways, this is only the beginning.

You've walked through prophecies, promises, and warnings. You've heard the call to watch and be ready, and been reminded of the unshakable hope we have in Jesus. The message of the End-Times isn't meant to paralyze us with fear—it's meant to awaken us to faith. To urgency. To holy living. To hope that refuses to die, even in the darkest days.

The return of Christ is not just a doctrine to believe—it's a reality to live for.

So now what?

Live with eyes lifted. Not in escapism, but in expectation.
Live with a heart anchored. Not in this world, but in God's unchanging Word.
Live with hands ready. Not clinging to comfort, but serving with courage and compassion.

The world is groaning. The signs are intensifying. But our hope is not in headlines or timelines—it's in the One who holds time in

His hands. He is coming soon. And until that day, we are called to shine like lights, speak the truth in love, and endure with faith that overcomes.

Hold fast. Stay awake. Don't lose heart.

Because the One who promised is faithful.

*"Now may the God of hope fill you with all joy and peace in believing, so that by the power of the Holy Spirit you may abound in hope."*— Romans 15:13 (ESV)

**Maranatha. Come, Lord Jesus!**

*Also by BiblePlan Devotionals*

# Freedom Fighters:
# Heroes of Faith Who Stood for Truth

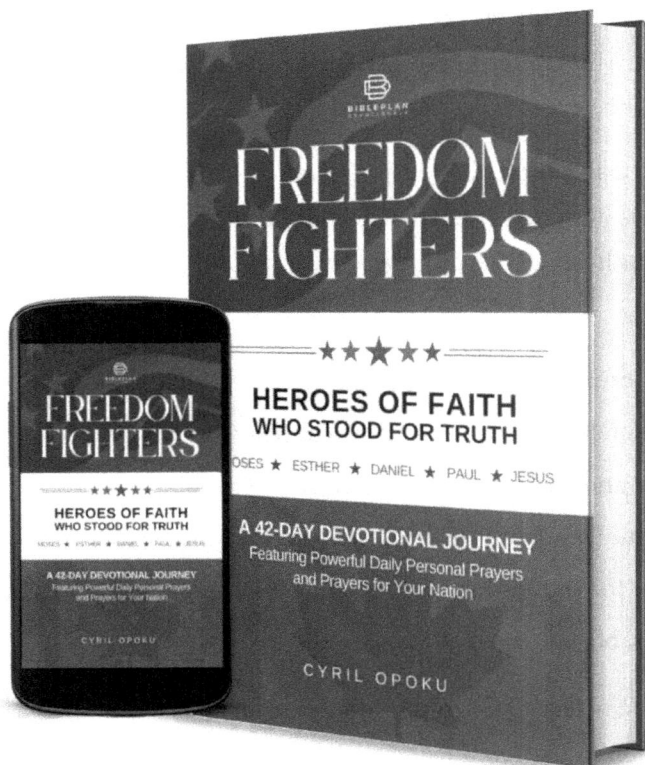

**A 42-Day Devotional Journey with Powerful Daily Prayers—for You and Your Nation!**

What does real courage look like in a world that silences truth? How do you stand firm when everything around you tells you to compromise?

*Freedom Fighters: Heroes of Faith Who Stood for Truth* is a powerful 42-day devotional that explores the lives of five extraordinary biblical figures—**Moses, Esther, Daniel, Paul, and Jesus**—each of whom stood boldly for truth in the face of fear, injustice, and opposition. Their stories weren't safe. They weren't easy. But they were full of purpose—and they're more relevant now than ever.

This devotional is more than just inspiration—it's a **call to action**. Each daily entry is designed to challenge your faith, strengthen your resolve, and stir your heart to live courageously in today's culture. You'll walk through:

- ✅ **Daily Scripture Readings** built around key Bible passages
- ✅ **Deep Reflections** rooted in timeless truth
- ✅ **Ponder and Reflection Questions** for spiritual growth
- ✅ **Powerful Personal Prayers** to help you respond in faith
- ✅ **Prayers for the Nation** to intercede for your country and community
- ✅ **Memorable Quotes** that inspire bold living

Whether you're leading a group, studying alone, or looking for a meaningful gift, *Freedom Fighters* will help you discover what it means to live for something greater than yourself.

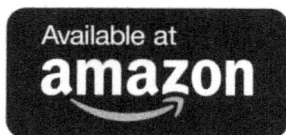

Available at
**amazon**

www.ingramcontent.com/pod-product-compliance
Lightning Source LLC
Chambersburg PA
CBHW060422050426
42449CB00009B/2094